RAINBOW CARAVAN PARK

by
Gwen Berwick and Sydney Thorne

Cornelsen

Rainbow Caravan Park

Gwen Berwick, Sydney Thorne

Verlagsredaktion
Sandhya Gupta

Technische Umsetzung
Peter Richter

Umschlagfoto
Shutterstock Images LLC,
photobank.ch (oben links), Atlaspix

Illustration
Kay Dixey, Linda Rogers Associates

www.cornelsen.de

1. Auflage, 3. Druck 2009

Druck: CS-Druck CornelsenStürtz, Berlin

ISBN 978-3-464-34394-4

Inhalt gedruckt auf säurefreiem Papier aus nachhaltiger Forstwirtschaft.

CONTENTS

Chapter Five 26

CHAPTER ONE

"Don't be silly, Mum!" said Lorna. "Of course I packed my jeans!"

"Well, it's easy to forget things, Lorna," said Lorna's mother, Mrs Stokes. She was sitting next to Lorna, and was driving the car. "Especially when you're away from home for so long for the first time. Did you pack enough socks?"

"Mum! I'm almost eighteen!"

Lorna Stokes looked out of the window. She had just finished her first year at York College. And now she was on her way to her first summer job away from home. A job in a caravan park …

Lorna lived in York, but she had found a job for six weeks at the Rainbow Caravan Park, a few miles outside Scarborough. And today her mother and her older brother, Matthew, were taking her there.

Lorna felt excited. What would the caravan park be like? Would there be a swimming-pool? And tennis courts? Would the customers be nice? The caravan park was near the sea: would she have time to go down to the beach? Mrs Croft, the caravan park manager, had sounded nice on the phone.

"You'll have a great summer!" said Lorna's brother, Matthew. He was sitting behind his mother. "Working in a caravan is easy! A bit of cleaning, a bit of washing up in the café – and then you'll spend the afternoon on the beach. You'll even have your own caravan, won't you? And in the evenings, I bet you'll be at the disco with the guys from the caravan park. Call it a job? More like a paid holiday, if you ask me!"

"Well, I'm sure I'll have to work sometimes!" laughed Lorna. She liked her brother Matthew, who was two years older than her. Matthew was on holiday from his college in Sheffield.

"We'll soon be able to see the sea!" said Mrs Stokes. "You packed your swimming things, didn't you, Lorna?"
"Mum! I'm not a baby!"
"Do you remember the caravan that we had in Devon a few years ago?" went on Mrs Stokes. "That was a beautiful place. Just a few caravans in a field. Big old trees, and the path going down to the sea."
"The tennis was great," said Matthew. "And there was that guy with his new motorbike, and ..."
But his mother interrupted him.
"Oh no!" she said. "There's a sea mist over Scarborough!"

It was true. Behind them it was sunny, but in front of them everything was grey. It suddenly felt cold, even inside the car. Suddenly, too, everybody stopped talking. It began to rain.

"Mrs Croft said you turn right soon after the sports centre in Seamer," said Lorna.
"I thought your caravan park was in Scarborough," said Matthew.
"It's a bit outside," said Lorna. "About five miles."
"Let's hope there's a bus into Scarborough!" said Matthew. "There's nothing to do in Seamer. And five miles is a long way when you're walking!"
They drove past some small factories. The caravan park was at the end of the road.
Mrs Stokes parked the car outside the caravan park office. "Well, here we are!" she said.

Lorna knew that her mother was trying to sound happy – but really she wasn't happy at all.

The Caravan Park was a flat field with two long lines of grey-green caravans. The caravans all looked the same, and were very near each other. There were no trees. The toilet block had

a broken window. The café was a grey building with a dirty yellow door. Nothing in the caravan park was beautiful or attractive.
There was nobody in the caravan park office. But there was a note on the door:

Welcome to our Caravan Park, Lorna!
Sorry I'm out. Your caravan is the yellow one,
the last one on the right when you leave the
office. It's open: go in and make yourself at home.
I'll see you when I come back.
Mrs Croft

Lorna, Matthew and Mrs Stokes walked past the long line of caravans. It was still raining. A few people looked at them through the windows of the caravans.

"That must be your caravan, Lorna," said Mrs Stokes. "It's green, not yellow, but it's nice and big. You ..."
"No, Mum. There's one more caravan in this line," said Matthew.
Behind the last big caravan was a very small, yellow one. They went into it and Lorna put her bag down. The bag wasn't big, but it looked big in the little caravan. It was cold, and there was the smell of a room that has been empty for many weeks.

It was awful. Mrs Stokes didn't even try to sound happy any more.
"Lorna," she said. "This is terrible. Are you sure ...?"
"Mum, it's OK!" said Lorna. "I don't need a big caravan: a small one is much nicer, really. I can soon tidy it a bit."

Lorna was almost crying. But she was trying hard to sound happy.
"I don't like to leave you here, alone," said Mrs Stokes.
"Don't worry about me, Mum! I can look after myself!" said Lorna.
"And you'll be here on your 18th birthday!" went on Mrs Stokes. "Your birthday will be your last day here, won't it? Are you sure you couldn't come home one day earlier?"
"Don't be silly, Mum!" said Lorna. "I won't be alone. Do you remember my friend Sarah, from college? Well, she lives in Scarborough. So I'll go and see her."

"Lorna," said Matthew, as they walked back to the car. "I'll come one day on my new motorbike and see you."
"That'll be great!" said Lorna.
Lorna kissed her mother and Matthew. She smiled and waved as they drove away.

Then she turned back towards her caravan. She felt very much alone.

CHAPTER TWO

Vrrroooom!
At first, Lorna thought that Matthew had come back to the caravan park, on his motorbike! It sounded very much like his bike!

Lorna opened the door of her caravan. Outside, she saw an 18 year old boy, of Asian origin. He had just arrived on his motorbike. He had stopped outside a small caravan, a bit like Lorna's, at the end of the line of caravans on the other side of the field.

The boy waved when he saw her, and came over to her caravan. He was very good-looking.

"Hi, I'm Ashraf," he said. "You must be Lorna. It's good to see you. I work here, too – and I can tell you: there's more than enough work for two people! It's my free afternoon today, so I've been out on my motorbike."
"Oh, er ... Come inside, you'll get wet," said Lorna. "I haven't met anybody here yet. I only arrived a few minutes ago. Mrs Croft is out."
"Not surprising!" said Ashraf.
"Look," said Lorna, "Shall I make a cup of tea? Perhaps I can find some tea in one of these cupboards ..."
"There won't be any food or drink in your cupboards!" said Ashraf. "Not if I know Mrs Croft. But I'll see you in the café in a few minutes. We can have a drink there, and I can show you where everything is."

UITS

When Lorna went into the café a few minutes later, it was empty. She sat down at one of the tables.
Then the door opened, and Ashraf came in.
"Are you waiting for a waitress?" he laughed. "You're the waitress now, Lorna! Come into the kitchen."

Lorna felt a bit stupid. But Ashraf was very friendly, and she soon felt better again. She followed him through a door into the kitchen. It was very small.
"This is where we work," explained Ashraf. "The microwave is over there. Plates, cups and glasses are up here, and knives, forks and spoons are in here. Frying pans are over there. And this is the dishwasher. But when things get very busy, you often have to wash up by hand. It's faster."
"Have you been here long?" asked Lorna.
"I started here in June," said Ashraf. "Now come on, let's make a cup of tea."

They were drinking their tea when a large woman walked into the kitchen. She had brown hair and long green earrings.
"No, don't get up," she said. "I'm Sheila Croft. Welcome to our little family here at the Rainbow Caravan Park. I'm very happy to see you, Laura. Did you have a good journey?"
"Lorna, not Laura," said Lorna. "But ..."
She saw Ashraf laughing when Mrs Croft talked about the 'little family'. But Mrs Croft didn't see him, and went on talking.
"Did you find your caravan easily?"
But again, Lorna didn't have time to answer.
Mrs Croft looked at Ashraf and his cup of tea, and then she looked at the clock.

"When you've finished your break, Ashraf," she said, "you can start preparing tonight's dinner. You can show Laura where everything is. And ..."

"Lorna, not Laura," said Ashraf.

"Yes," said Mrs Croft, without stopping. "And if you need help, Laura, you can always ask me. You'll usually find me in the office."

She went to the door.

"I know that teenagers are lazy, and often a bit stupid. But you'll have to work hard here, Laura."

And with that, Mrs Croft went out of the kitchen.

Lorna was shocked. How could Mrs Croft say things like that about teenagers?

"Hm, you'll be lucky if you can find Mrs Croft in the office!" said Ashraf. "You've had your friendly welcome: now the hard work can begin! You wash this salad and cut the tomatoes. I'll do the chips."

Ashraf was right: it was hard work. There was so much work in the first few days that Lorna didn't have time to think. In the morning she helped to make breakfast for thirty to forty people. She took the orders when the customers came into the café: some wanted sausage and tomato, some wanted bacon and tomato, some wanted egg and bacon, and others wanted bacon and sausage and egg ... It was so difficult to remember who wanted what!

After breakfast, Lorna and Ashraf had to wash up and clean the tables and the café floor. Then they had to empty the rubbish bins and clean the showers and the toilets in the toilet block. And when that was finished, it was time to prepare lunch. There were more customers for lunch than for breakfast, because some people came to the café from outside the caravan park.

There was more work in the afternoon, too. If she was lucky, she went shopping for food in the big supermarket near the caravan park. It was always good to get out of the caravan park: sometimes Lorna could even sit down for a moment! One of the worst jobs, Lorna found, was cutting the grass near the caravans. It made the customers angry because it was so noisy, and sometimes the customers shouted at her. Lorna was surprised how grumpy the customers were. They were on holiday, but they never seemed to smile.

In the evening, Ashraf and Lorna were back in the kitchen, preparing and serving the evening meal. They cooked everything in fat: the sausages, the chicken pieces, the fish. Lorna soon hated the smell of fat. The smell soon got into her clothes and her hair.

After they washed up after the evening meal, Ashraf and Lorna had to wash up again, clean the café tables and chairs, and clean everything in the kitchen. And often, when they had finished, Mrs Croft still found more work to do for them. And when Lorna went to bed at last, the customers had used all the hot water and the water was cold!

Lorna soon found that she worked such long hours that she had no time to visit her friend Sarah. She had one free afternoon each week, but she was too tired to travel five miles to Scarborough. But at least Ashraf was there, and he was great fun.

Ashraf tried to help Lorna as much as he could, and they often laughed together – especially when Lorna made mistakes. Once, a customer ordered a ham salad.

"Do you like uncooked ham, Lorna?" Ashraf asked her later that day.

"Uncooked ham? Why? What do you mean?" asked Lorna.

"Well, you made that man's salad with the uncooked ham, not the cooked ham!" said Ashraf, and he laughed.

"Oh no!" said Lorna. "How stupid! Do you think he'll be ill? Do you think he'll die?"

Ashraf laughed. "Don't be silly," he said. He put his arm on her shoulder. "He'll be OK."
Lorna looked up at Ashraf and smiled. His arm felt good on her shoulder. Suddenly, Ashraf took his arm away.
"Back to work!" he said.

Sometimes Lorna made Ashraf laugh by giving orders and talking like Mrs Croft. Once, Lorna was doing this when Mrs Croft walked into the kitchen. Lorna hoped that Mrs Croft hadn't heard her!

Lorna didn't see Mrs Croft very often. She came into the kitchen before breakfast or before lunch to tell them what they had to do. And sometimes she came to say that somebody was on the phone for Ashraf in the office. "Ashraf, it's that girl again for you," she often said, and Lorna wondered who 'that girl' was.

Lorna liked Ashraf, and soon she learned a little more about him. He was from Bradford, a large town in the north of England, near Leeds. He lived in a part of Bradford where many people were of Asian origin. He was doing a course in photography at a college in Bradford. Like Lorna, he was working at the Rainbow Caravan Park in his college holidays. He liked watching the people in the caravan park. Sometimes he took photos of them. It was a project for college, he said.

Sometimes Lorna saw that Ashraf was looking at her. When she looked back, he always turned away, quickly.
"He has beautiful dark brown eyes," thought Lorna. "But what does he think of me? Am I like all the other people here, or does he think I'm special?"

CHAPTER THREE

"Two teas, one sausage, bacon and egg, and two bread and butter. Brown bread!"

It was 9.00 am, an especially busy time in the kitchen. Ashraf was cooking the food; Lorna took the orders, brought the customers their food and then brought the dirty plates and mugs back into the kitchen.

"It's your free afternoon tomorrow, Lorna, isn't it?" asked Ashraf. "What are you going to do?"

"My brother Matthew is coming over to see me from York," said Lorna. "That's if I'm not too tired! Look, I'll take the two teas and the bread and butter to table 7. Can you bring the sausage, bacon and egg, Ashraf?"

"OK. I'll bring them in a moment," answered Ashraf.

Lorna smiled at the man and woman who were sitting at table 7. She carefully put the tea and the plates on their table.

"Two teas, and two bread and butter," she said. "Your cooked breakfast will be here in a moment."

But the man looked angry.

"I ordered brown bread!" he said. "You've brought white bread!"

"Oh, I'm sorry," answered Lorna, quickly. "Look, I'll take it back to the kitchen. I can easily bring you brown bread."

But the man wasn't listening.

"It's that Pakistani boy in the kitchen, isn't it?" he went on. "These immigrants aren't used to work, are they? They're lazy, all of them."

At that moment, Ashraf arrived with the cooked breakfast. Lorna hoped he hadn't heard the man.
"One sausage, bacon and egg. Is this for you, sir?" said Ashraf.

"Yes, it is!" shouted the man. "And I hope this order is right! You immigrants still have to learn so much! Why they've given you a job here, I just don't know!"
Ashraf looked at the man coldly. Then he turned back to the kitchen without saying anything.

When Lorna came back into the kitchen, she was furious. "Why didn't you say anything to that awful man?" she said to Ashraf. "It was terrible. How could he say things like that?" Ashraf was washing up some plates. He didn't answer for a moment.

"It happens all the time," he said. "You get used to it ... No, that's not right. You never get used to it. But you learn to say nothing and to walk away."

"But that's the wrong thing to do!" said Lorna. "If you always walk away, people like that will never learn! You should tell him he's a racist. You should tell him he's not allowed to talk like that! "

Ashraf turned to look at Lorna.

"Oh yes, it's easy for you to talk like that, isn't it?" he said. "You live in a nice part of York. I bet there aren't any Asian people there, or very few. And I bet there aren't any gangs of young men on the streets at night, are there?"

Lorna had never heard Ashraf talk like this before. He sounded different. His eyes were very angry.

"You've never seen violence, have you, Lorna? I know what it's like. Gangs sometimes called me terrible names when I went to school. They shouted 'Go home to Pakistan'! They had knives. And do you really think I could say 'Excuse me. You're racists. You're not allowed to talk like that'?"

"I'm sorry, Ashraf," said Lorna. "It's true, what you say. I was only trying to help, and ..."

"Forget it, OK?" said Ashraf. "Here's the last order. Three sausage, egg and tomato for table 5. Can you take it to table 5? I'll start clearing away in here, and ..."

At that moment Mrs Croft came into the kitchen.

"Telephone for you, Ashraf," she said. "That girl again. Can't you ask her to call when it's less busy here?"

Ashraf left the kitchen.
"And Lorna," went on Mrs Croft, "when you've finished in the kitchen, can you empty all the bins next to each caravan? And then you can start cleaning the toilet block."
Mrs Croft walked out of the kitchen, and Lorna took the food to table 5.
"Well," she thought, "at least Mrs Croft has learnt my name now!"

While she was clearing away in the kitchen, Lorna thought about Ashraf. She often thought about Ashraf. She liked him. Well, it was more than that, really: she couldn't stop thinking of him. It felt good when she was with him. She liked talking with him. And he was very good-looking.
But what did he think of her? She didn't really know. He was friendly, and sometimes he seemed to like her very much. But when she looked at him, he often turned away.
"He's like a closed book," she thought. "I can't read him!"
And then Lorna wondered: "Who is the girl on the phone?"

At that moment, Ashraf came back into the kitchen. He didn't look happy.
"Thanks for starting to clear away," he said. And he started to load the dishwasher.
They were both quiet for a moment, and then Lorna asked, "Who is the girl that phones you, Ashraf?"
"None of your business!" answered Ashraf, grumpily. "Anyway," he added, "if you really want to know, it's my sister."

CHAPTER FOUR

The next morning, Mrs Croft said: "Lorna, I have to go into town. Will you clean the office while I'm away? And answer the phone if it rings, Lorna. Ashraf is working outside this morning."

Lorna began to tidy the office. And about half an hour later, the telephone rang.

"Hallo. Can I speak with Ashraf Ahmed, please?" said a voice. It was a girl's voice.

"Wait a moment," answered Lorna. She put the phone down, and went to find Ashraf. She felt annoyed. It was bad enough that Ashraf's sister phoned so often. Now she had to deliver messages too!

Ashraf was also annoyed when he answered the phone.

"Not now," he said. "I'll call you this evening, if I have time … No … No! … Well, I'm sorry: I can't talk now!"

And he put the phone down.

"Why doesn't your sister phone you on your mobile?" asked Lorna.

"Well, er …," he began. "Um … Phoning a mobile is expensive. And she doesn't have much money. So it's cheaper to phone the office. And anyway: it's none of your business!"

"OK, OK, I only asked," said Lorna. She wondered why Ashraf was always so annoyed after his sister phoned. But this was not the right moment to ask more questions.

Matthew arrived after lunch. Lorna was just finishing her work in the kitchen when she heard his motorbike. When she

came outside, she found that Matthew and Ashraf were already talking about motorbikes.
"Nice bike, that!" Ashraf was saying.
"Thanks," said Matthew. "And is that your bike over there? It's nice."
"Yes, it's mine," said Ashraf. "It's OK. Not as good as a Racer! That's what I'd really like!"
"Yes, or a Pasawaki. That's my favourite bike!" said Matthew. "Oh, there you are Lorna!" he went on. "I've just met Ashraf and seen his motorbike. Now, come on: let's go into Scarborough. It's not even raining!"
"Lorna can have my helmet, if you want," said Ashraf.
"Thanks," said Matthew, "But I've brought a helmet for her."

It was good to leave the caravan park for a few hours. Lorna felt so free with her brother. In Scarborough, they went to the castle. Then they walked down into the town and saw the little fishing boats. They chatted a lot. Lorna told Matthew about her work and about life in the caravan park. She told him about the customers, and Mrs Croft, and the kitchen, and all the other work. And about Ashraf.

Then they went into a café for an ice-cream.
"You like Ashraf very much, don't you?" said Matthew, just as Lorna put a big spoonful of ice-cream into her mouth. Lorna went very red.
"Oh, I don't know," she said, without looking at her brother. "He's very friendly, but …"
"It doesn't worry you that he's Asian?" asked Matthew. "No, don't look at me like that, Lorna. I'm not going to say awful things about Asians. You know me better than that. But going

out with an Asian boy – or girl – has its own problems, you know."

"Well, you should know!"said Lorna. "What about your girlfriend Amina?"

Matthew had met Amina at college in Sheffield. They had gone out together for nearly a year. And Lorna had met her when Amina had come to York with Matthew.

"I was thinking of Amina," said Matthew, looking a bit sad. "Do you know why it finished, between Amina and me?"

"No, I never asked," said Lorna quietly. She suddenly felt a bit cold. "And you never said anything."

"It wasn't easy for Amina or me," said Matthew, playing with his long ice-cream spoon. "At first we talked a lot, we had lots of fun together, we had a good time. Then we started going out together. But her parents didn't like it and my friends weren't very happy about it."

Matthew looked at Lorna.

"Her parents wanted Amina to come home to them at weekends. They were worried she would grow away from them. She was now living a very different lifestyle. So Amina was torn between them and us. My friends would never take her seriously. They often asked her stupid questions like 'Does your father sleep on a bed of nails?' and so on. Sometimes I didn't want my friends to see us together. It was all too much for her. One day, she left college, without telling us. She never phoned, and she never answered my letters. I never heard from her again."

Matthew was quiet for a moment, and Lorna looked down at the table.

"That can happen in all families," she said.

"I know. Of course," said Matthew. "Look, Lorna, I'm not trying to tell you what to do. I'm just telling you what happened to me."

"Yes," said Lorna, more softly. "Thanks, Matthew. It's not easy for you to talk about Amina, I can see that."

"Perhaps you'll be luckier," smiled Matthew. "I hope so. Anyway, it's time to go back. If we're late, Mrs Croft will throw a frying pan at you!"

Matthew and Lorna drove back to the Rainbow Caravan Park on Matthew's bike. Lorna felt a bit sad when Matthew had to leave.

"Look, I don't need two motorbike helmets," said Matthew. "I'll leave this one here, then you can go out with Ashraf on his bike."

"I don't think he'll ask me," said Lorna.

"Well, you never know!" said Matthew. And he smiled. "Bye, Lorna. Good luck!"

At that moment, the phone rang in the office. Nobody answered it. It rang and rang.

"I don't know where Mrs Croft is," said Lorna. "I think I should answer it. Bye, Matthew! Give my love to Mum!"

Then she ran to the phone.

"Rainbow Caravan Park, good evening," she said.

"Hallo, could I speak with Ashraf Ahmed?"

It was Ashraf's sister again.

"I'm sorry," said Lorna. "Your brother isn't here."

There was a short pause. And then the voice said:

"What do you mean, my brother? Ashraf is my boyfriend."

CHAPTER FIVE

"So who is she, Ashraf?"

It was the question that Lorna wanted to ask all morning. But first she was too busy in the kitchen, and then Ashraf went with Mrs Croft to Scarborough to do some shopping. Lunch was so busy that Mrs Croft worked in the kitchen, too – and of course Lorna didn't want to say anything in front of her.
But when Mrs Croft left the kitchen and Lorna and Ashraf were alone, the question came out like a rocket.

"What are you talking about, Lorna?" said Ashraf.
"That girl who phones you almost every day! I felt really stupid when I said her brother wasn't here – and then she said you were her boyfriend! At least I know what the true situation is!"
"What did she say?" asked Ashraf.
"What do you think? Look, Ashraf, if you have a girlfriend in Bradford, that's none of my business, I know. But I thought we were friends. I thought that perhaps you liked me. I didn't think you told me things which weren't true!"
"Lorna, it's not like that … not what you think," said Ashraf. "If you give me a chance, I'll …"
"Like you said, Ashraf," said Lorna, "it's none of my business!"
And Lorna slammed the kitchen door, went back to her caravan and cried.

Lorna and Ashraf didn't talk much together that day. But when they finished work in the evening, Ashraf said, "Sit down for a moment, Lorna. I'd like to talk with you."

His voice was tired, but it was warm and friendly too, and Lorna sat down.

"Look, I want to explain about the phone calls," said Ashraf. "It's true. Raheema isn't my sister. She was my girlfriend. Was my girlfriend, Lorna, but isn't my girlfriend any more. I … I didn't want to talk about her. I didn't want to think about her. That's why I said she was my sister."

"Ashraf," said Lorna, "you don't have to tell me anything if you don't want to."

"No, I'd like to explain everything. You see, Lorna, I wanted to get away from her. That's why I took this summer job far away from Bradford. I didn't give her the phone number here and I changed my mobile number. But Raheema talked with a friend of mine and he told her the name of the caravan park. Then she found out the phone number."

"She must like … love you a lot," said Lorna. It wasn't easy for her to say it.

"She doesn't love me!" said Ashraf. "We started going out together two years ago. Then last year she suddenly left me. And I found out that she was going out with another guy. I felt awful. Then, she was suddenly nice again and wanted to go out with me again. I was stupid and said 'yes'."

Ashraf stopped, and Lorna looked at him.

"A few weeks ago, she left me a second time – and again for another guy. Now she's finished with him, and she wants me again. But I know her tricks now! I don't want to see her. She has hurt me twice, and I don't want her to hurt me again. I don't want to go out with her. I don't want to go out with any girl!"

"OK, I get the message," said Lorna.

And that was that, thought Lorna, when she was in bed in her caravan that night. Ashraf wanted to be alone. He wasn't interested in going out with a girl. So he wasn't interested in her. Well, at least she knew what the situation was. That should make it easier for her, she told herself.

But Lorna didn't sleep well that night.

CHAPTER SIX

A few days passed. Lorna and Ashraf were friendly with each other. But Lorna tried not be with him, alone, too often.

One Tuesday morning, there was a crisis in the kitchen: the dishwasher didn't work any more. Ashraf and Lorna had to wash up all the plates and cups, all the knives, forks and spoons by hand. When they had finished, Mrs Croft came into the kitchen. She didn't look happy.

"Somebody can come to repair the dishwasher," she said. "But he can only come at lunchtime, and he said it could take two or three hours. And we can't cook meals while he's working. So I'll have to close the café. It'll be an expensive day for me!"

She went to the kitchen door.

"Oh," she added, "Ashraf and Lorna, I'll give you your free afternoons today. That way you can work full days when the dishwasher is working again. That will be OK, won't it?"

And she was out of the kitchen before they could answer.

"Well, thank you, Mrs Croft!" said Lorna, in her Mrs Croft voice.

Ashraf laughed. Lorna loved it when he laughed like that.

"Great!" he said. "A free afternoon, and it's nice and sunny, too. I'd like to ride my bike out on the Moors and take some photos."

And then, to Lorna's surprise, he added: "I wish you could come too, Lorna, but I only have one helmet."

"Well, I have a motorbike helmet." said Lorna. "Matthew left me one of his. But if you want to go alone, Ashraf, …"

"No, let's go together," said Ashraf. And he smiled. "It would be great to get away from this place for an afternoon!"

Tuesday afternoon was warm and sunny. Lorna sat on the motorbike, behind Ashraf, with her arms around him. Ashraf took the little roads into the Moors. The hills looked flat when

you were on them, but the roads down into the valleys were very steep – 30% sometimes! Going fast down these roads was exciting!

Ashraf had his camera with him. From time to time he stopped and took photos. He took photos of strange things, thought Lorna. A rock with the sun on it. A leaf that was just starting to go yellow. "These photos will be great for my next project at college," he said.

Later in the afternoon they stopped near a little river. Lorna took her helmet off. It was good to feel the sun on her face. She lay down on the warm grass. Life felt good.

"Ashraf," she said. "You know I have a friend from college who lives in Scarborough – Sarah. Well, she phoned me a few days ago and invited me to a disco in Scarborough on Saturday evening. I'm going back home in three weeks," she added, "and I'd like to see Sarah before I leave."

Lorna hadn't dared to ask Ashraf to come with her before. Now it seemed right to ask him

"Would you like to come to the disco, too, Ashraf?"

He smiled.

"Thanks, Lorna," he said. "I'd like to come. We can go on my bike."

"Thanks for the trip, Ashraf," said Lorna, when they arrived back at the caravan park. She squeezed his hand and gave him a quick kiss. "It was good fun. We must do it again. It's good to get away from …"

"Ah, there you are at last!" said Mrs Croft. "I need you to prepare two caravans for some new customers. They're arriving tomorrow morning."

"But you said we could have our free afternoons today!" protested Lorna.
"Lorna," said Mrs Croft. "We're one family here. I've done all the work here this afternoon, and now my back is hurting. Is it too much to ask you to help me, now that you're back here?"

Lorna helped Ashraf clean the caravans, but she was furious. And that night, when they said good night to each other, Lorna said:
"It's not fair, Ashraf. We never get the breaks that we should. And if we work extra hours, Mrs Croft should pay us more, shouldn't she? We should go and talk with her. We should ask her for more money."
"When?" said Ashraf.
"Look, there's a light on in the office. She must be there now. So let's go now!"
"Do you think it will work?"
"I don't know," said Lorna. "But we can try!"

Mrs Croft looked surprised when Lorna and Ashraf walked into the office. And Lorna felt very nervous. Talking with Ashraf was easy. Talking with Mrs Croft was different.
"Ashraf and I work lots of extra hours here," began Lorna. "And we often don't get our breaks. That's fine, but we think that you should pay us for these extra hours. We feel that …"
"Lorna," interrupted Mrs Croft. "Working in the real world isn't like working in college! People have to work hard, and …"
"We enjoy the work," said Lorna. "But it's only fair to pay us for the extra work that we do."
"We're here because we're trying to earn money for college," added Ashraf.

"Well, Ashraf never complained before you came, Lorna," said Mrs Croft.

"Well, perhaps he's used to it," said Lorna. "Asians are used to working hard. I know that. But I'm not!"

But when she said this, Ashraf turned to her angrily. Something was wrong. "I think it's great, Ashraf. All the little Indian food shops, open all hours of the day and night. Big families: the children helping the parents in the shop. Everybody so happy. I think it's ..."

But Ashraf was now really angry.

"How dare you say that?" he shouted at Lorna.

Lorna couldn't understand him.

"What's wrong?" she asked. "I didn't say anything horrible. I only said that Asians are used to hard work. What's wrong with that?"

"I think you're both a bit tired," said Mrs Croft, with a smile. "Perhaps we should all go to bed. We can talk about this another time."

Lorna and Ashraf left the office without speaking. But when they were outside, Ashraf said:

"I didn't think you were a racist, Lorna!"

Lorna was furious, too.

"I can't understand you, Ashraf!" she shouted. "But I didn't think you could be so stupid! I bet you made Mrs Croft very happy. She won't pay us any more money now, will she? You've ruined our chances, Ashraf!"

"You've ruined more than that, Lorna!" said Ashraf. And he went back to his caravan.

CHAPTER SEVEN

When Lorna came into the kitchen the next morning, she was still angry. She didn't say "Hallo" to Ashraf when he walked in. And he didn't even look at her.

It wasn't a good morning. The customers were grumpy. Lorna ran in and out of the kitchen with the full plates. Of course, she dropped one: the plate broke, and she had to pick up the egg and tomato from the floor.

"Why didn't you help me?" she shouted at Ashraf, when she put the broken pieces of the plate into the bin.
"Well, you see, I'm so 'hard-working', like 'all Asians'," said Ashraf. "So of course I didn't hear you. I was too busy!"

Lorna and Ashraf tried to work in different places that week. And when they had to be together, they tried not to talk with each other.

Lorna wondered about the disco on Saturday. She wanted to see Sarah. But she didn't want to go with Ashraf now. But the problem was that she had no other transport. There were no buses on a Saturday evening, and a taxi would be so expensive. And she didn't want to walk five miles at night! No, it was better to go with Ashraf. She wouldn't have to talk with him.

Lorna wondered if Ashraf would say he couldn't go to the disco. But he didn't say anything, so on Saturday evening they went together to the disco in Scarborough, on Ashraf's motorbike. But they didn't speak.

The disco was in a club in the centre of Scarborough. Lorna could hear the music from outside. Inside, the club was full of young people. Some were dancing, others were chatting, in groups, at the tables. Lorna soon found Sarah, and chatted happily with Sarah and her friends. They laughed a lot, and

Lorna began to enjoy herself. She soon forgot the Rainbow Caravan Park and her problems with Ashraf.

Later in the evening, Lorna saw Ashraf dancing with a girl with long fair hair. She was a bit surprised. He was flirting with her. "Well, none of my business," thought Lorna.

At the end of the evening, Ashraf was still with the same girl.
"I could take you home on my motorbike, Tara," he said to her. "I can come back for Lorna later."
"Well, you can show me your bike, if you like," said the girl, "but I'll walk home, thanks."
And they went outside together.

Later, Lorna said goodbye to Sarah and her friends. They left the club, and then Lorna went to find Ashraf. She looked everywhere, but she couldn't find him. Then she saw the girl with the long fair hair, so she asked her where Ashraf was.
"Oh," said the girl. "I saw him drive away on his motorbike. He told me he was going back to the place where he's working – it's a campsite, I think."

Lorna couldn't believe it. Ashraf had gone back without her! But he had promised to take her home!
And what could she do now? Sarah and her friends had gone home. There were no buses, and she didn't have enough money for a taxi.
There was only one thing to do. She walked the five long miles back to the caravan park. It was a long, cold walk. It was dark, and it started to rain. Lorna got wetter and wetter – and angrier and angrier.

It was nearly two hours later when Lorna arrived at the caravan park. She was wet to the skin. And she was furious. She went to Ashraf's caravan, and hammered on his door. She waited a few moments, and then she hammered again. Ashraf opened the door. Lorna went into his caravan.

"Why did you come back without me?" she shouted. "How could you do a horrible thing like that?"

Lorna was trembling, and Ashraf put his pullover on her shoulders. But his voice was hard when he answered.

"What's wrong?" he said. "Tara said she prefers walking. So of course I thought that 'all' white girls prefer walking!"

"Don't be stupid, Ashraf!" said Lorna. "Tara probably lives near the disco. I had to walk five miles or more."

"Well, I just thought that 'all' white people are the same, just like 'all' Asians are the same," said Ashraf.

Lorna stared at him.

"Ashraf, what are you talking about? I just can't understand you. What's the problem? Tell me. We can't go on like this!"

Ashraf looked at the table between them.

"I just didn't think you were like the others," he said. "I thought you were different. But you're racist, too. It was a shock when I found out."

"That's not fair, Ashraf," said Lorna. "I'm not racist! I think it's awful when people say horrible things about Asians. How can you say I'm racist? I like you, don't I? Well, I liked you till a few days ago. How could I like you if I was racist?"

"That's a really silly argument," said Ashraf. "Of course you can be racist and like somebody who has a different colour."

"Silly argument?" shouted Lorna. "Well, what is a racist, then?!"

"All people are individuals, aren't they? And we're all different, aren't we? We all have our own opinions, our own feelings, don't we? Well, you're racist when you stop thinking about people as individuals! You're racist when you think that 'all' Asians do this and 'all' Europeans do that! You're racist when you think that people with the same ethnic origin are all the same!"

Ashraf looked at Lorna.

"I thought you liked me – me, an individual called Ashraf! And then you started talking about 'all' Asians in their food shops. Do you think I live in a food shop, just because I'm Asian? Do you think I'm going to work in a food shop? If you think all Asians are the same, then you don't know *me* – Ashraf. I'm just 'an Asian', like all the others."

"You're talking nonsense, Ashraf!" Lorna shouted back. "You're annoyed because you don't get on with girls. Raheema left you. Tara didn't want to ride on your bike. And with me it's finished, too. Problems between girls and boys aren't new, Ashraf. And you can't say that the girls are racist just because they don't like you!"

"I never said that!" said Ashraf. He was angry. "You're not listening to what I'm saying!"

"Well, you're not listening to me!" said Lorna. "You left me at the disco, and that was a horrible thing to do! And now you're trying to say that I'm racist. I've had enough of this! I'm going to bed!"

And Lorna threw Ashraf's pullover on the floor, went out of the caravan, and slammed the door.

PHOTOGRAPHY

CHAPTER EIGHT

The next morning, Lorna felt tired and unhappy. Two more weeks in the caravan park! She wondered if she should go home now.

In the kitchen, Lorna and Ashraf didn't look at each other, and didn't speak.

"The sausages weren't really hot this morning," said one of the customers, when Lorna came to take away his dirty plate. It was Mr Griggs. He always ate sausages for breakfast, and he often complained about them. "A girl like you should know how to cook!"
"I didn't cook your sausages," said Lorna. "It was a man who cooked them."
"Ah, that's why they were cold," said Mr Griggs. "Say what you like, men can't cook. Cooking is a woman's job."
Lorna was shocked.
"Of course men can cook! Men cook in many of the best restaurants in the world!" she said.
But Mr Griggs wasn't listening to her. "Cooking is a woman's job," he said again. "Women are good at it; men aren't. Say what you like, all women should be at home, in the kitchen. That's where women belong."
Lorna felt tired and angry. She knew she should walk away. She knew that a waitress should never talk angrily with a customer. But now it didn't matter if she lost her job. She didn't really want to stay at the caravan park anyway.
So without thinking she said:

"That's not fair, Mr Griggs. It's a sexist argument."

"Sexist? What do you mean? I'm not sexist! Many of my friends are women!" answered Mr Griggs.

Lorna put the plate back on the table.

"All people are individuals, aren't they?" said Lorna. "And we're all different, aren't we? We all have our own opinions, our own feelings, don't we?"

Lorna felt that other customers in the café were looking at her now. But she had started, and she was going to say what she thought!

"You're sexist when you stop thinking about men or women as individuals! You're sexist when you think that 'all' men do this and 'all' women do that! You're sexist when you think that 'all' men like the same things, or 'all' women can do the same things!"

Lorna had spoken quickly, and Mr Griggs looked at her with surprise. He was so surprised that he began stirring his tea with his pen!

"But I'm sorry if your sausages were cold," finished Lorna. And with that, she turned and took the dirty plate back into the kitchen.

When Lorna came into the kitchen, she was still furious. But Ashraf was standing next to the dishwasher, laughing and laughing. Lorna stared at him.

"What's so funny?" she asked. She was annoyed.

"You ... You ..." began Ashraf. But he was laughing so much that he couldn't speak.

"What is it, Ashraf?" asked Lorna again. She was beginning to smile, now. Ashraf looked so funny.

"Don't you see, Lorna?" said Ashraf at last. "You were so angry with that man!"

"Well?"

"And you sounded just like me last night!" said Ashraf. "You used exactly the same words!"
"Just like ...?" Lorna thought for a moment.
"It's true! You're right, Ashraf!"
And Lorna started laughing too. It was good to laugh. Good to laugh with Ashraf. She felt so much better.
"I'm really sorry about last night, Ashraf," said Lorna.
"Forget it," said Ashraf. "I was stupid. And I was wrong to leave you at the disco. I'm sorry, Lorna."
He smiled at her.
"Let's be friends again," said Lorna. She gave him her hand. Ashraf took it and pulled her to him. Then he kissed her.

CHAPTER NINE

Lorna's last two weeks at the Rainbow Caravan Park were also her happiest. She and Ashraf spent all their free time together. They talked a lot and enjoyed being together. They laughed a lot, too, often about the most stupid things! And the work seemed easier: even Mr Griggs smiled at her when she brought him his sausages at breakfast.

In the evenings, after work, they sat in Ashraf's caravan. They talked and listened to music. In the candlelight, even the little caravan looked romantic!

Of course, the two weeks passed very quickly. And soon it was Friday, Lorna's last day at work. It was also her 18th birthday. Many of the customers had a card or a little present for her. And when Lorna had finished serving the breakfast, Ashraf said with a big smile:

"Close your eyes, Lorna! I have a surprise for you!"

And when she opened her eyes, there, on the kitchen table, was … a birthday cake!

"Happy birthday, Lorna! I made it last night!"

"Ashraf! You're so sweet!"

Lorna threw her arms around his neck. But just at that moment, the door opened, and Mrs Croft came in.

"The café floor is still dirty, and …" she began. Then she saw Lorna with her arms around Ashraf's neck.

She stopped, and didn't know what to say.

Then she saw the birthday cake.

"Oh, I forgot: Happy Birthday, Lorna!" she said. "I have something for you ... Come along to the office – when you've finished clearing everything away."

An hour later, Lorna was in Mrs Croft's office. First, Mrs Croft paid Lorna the money that she owed her.
"Thank you for your work, Lorna," she said. "You've helped a lot. And I have a birthday present for you, to say thank you. I know you've worked many extra ... er ... I know you've worked hard."
Lorna was surprised. Was Mrs Croft softer and friendlier than she thought? What could the present be? Some extra money, perhaps, for all the extra hours?
Mrs Croft gave Lorna a little parcel.
"Oh, thank you," said Lorna. "That's very kind of you, Mrs Croft."
It seemed wrong to open the present in front of Mrs Croft.
"Thank you," Lorna said again. "And thank you for my time here at the Rainbow Caravan Park."
"Well," said Mrs Croft, "you've worked hard. And Ashraf too. I'm surprised. I know that teenagers are lazy and stupid, and ..."
"That's not true!" said Lorna.
Mrs Croft looked at Lorna in surprise.
"What's not true?" she asked.
And Lorna thought: "I should really argue with Mrs Croft. I should tell her that all people are individuals. I should tell her that teenagers are not all the same ... But I don't want to waste my last few hours with Mrs Croft. I want to be with Ashraf."
"It doesn't matter," said Lorna. And she left the office.

"Well, what is it?" asked Ashraf. "A single sock? Or a broken torch with no batteries?"

They were in Lorna's caravan. Lorna had begun to pack her bag for her journey back to York.
"I thought it was perhaps some money ..." began Lorna.
"Money? From Mrs Croft?! Never!" said Ashraf, and they both laughed.
Lorna opened the parcel, and took out ... a plastic plate. It had a picture of Scarborough on it: the picture wasn't very good, and the colours were awful. The price was still on the plate.
Lorna stood up in the caravan, and said:
"Thank you, Mrs Croft! How very kind of you! I have worked at least fifty extra hours, and you have paid 89 pence on my present! I hope it hasn't made you ill!"
And then Lorna and Ashraf both laughed again.

After the evening meal, Ashraf and Lorna walked down to the beach. It was getting dark, and they were alone. They walked hand in hand next to the water. Sometimes they had to jump away when a wave came higher over the sand. And sometimes their feet got wet. But it didn't matter. Nothing mattered – except being together as long as they could, before Lorna left for York.
"What happened to Raheema?" asked Lorna. "She never phoned any more, did she?"
"No," said Ashraf. " I told her about you. I don't think I'll hear from her again."
"And what about your photography, Ashraf? Don't you want to take a few photos of the sun going down?"
Ashraf squeezed Lorna's hand. They stopped, and Ashraf looked into Lorna's eyes.
"No," he said. "I want to spend all these moments with you, Lorna. I love you."
He took her face in his hands, and they kissed.

The last morning passed as if in a dream. She said goodbye to all the customers.
“I’ll be good!” said Mr Griggs.

Then a quick goodbye in Mrs Croft's office.
"I hope you'll come again next summer?" asked Mrs Croft.
Lorna didn't answer.
And then Ashraf took Lorna to Scarborough station on his motorbike. "I'll come and see you in York on my way back to Bradford," he said. When the train left, Ashraf waved on the platform till Lorna couldn't see him any more.

Lorna felt sad, and happy, and very tired. When she closed her eyes, she was back on the beach with Ashraf, on their last evening together. When she opened her eyes again, the train had passed Malton. The sea was behind her. The caravan park was behind her. And Ashraf was behind her. And soon she would be in York. Matthew and her mother would be at the railway station.
What would she tell them? And what would her mother say when Lorna told her about Ashraf? What would her friends say? And what would Ashraf's parents say when he told them about her?
There were so many questions in her head!
And what about Ashraf? Would he really come and see her, as he had promised?

Could their love last? Lorna didn't know.
But she would try to make it work.

VOCABULARY

Abbreviations: *s.p.* = simple past (einfache Vergangenheit)
p.p. = past participle (Partizip Perfekt)
pl. = plural (Mehrzahl)

A

able [ebl]: (to) **be able to** können
(to) **add** [æd] hinzufügen
all: not ... at all überhaupt nicht
allowed [ə'laʊd]: (to) **be allowed to** dürfen
annoyed [ə'nɔɪd]: (to) **feel/be annoyed** verärgert sein
any: not ... any more nicht mehr
anyway ['eniweɪ] übrigens, jedenfalls
argument ['ɑːgjumənt] Argument
as als
at all: not ... at all überhaupt nicht
at last endlich
at the end [end] am Ende
awful ['ɔːfl] schrecklich, furchtbar

B

(to) **bet** [bet] wetten
bin [bɪn] Mülleimer
bit [bɪt]: **a bit** ein bisschen
block [blɒk] Gebäude
bread [bred] Brot
break [brek] Pause
broke [brəʊk]: *s.p.* (to) **break** zerbrechen
broken ['brəʊkən]: *p.p.* (to) **break** zerbrechen
business: none of your business das geht dich nichts an
butter ['bʌtə] Butter

C

candlelight ['kændllaɪt] Kerzenlicht
call [kɔːl]: **phone call** Telefonanruf
campsite ['kæmpsaɪt] Campingplatz
chance [tʃaːns] Chance, Gelegenheit
(to) **change** [tʃeɪndʒ] ändern
(to) **clear away** [klɪə] abräumen
college ['kɒlɪdʒ] Berufsschule; Fach(hoch)schule
(to) **come over** herüberkommen
(to) **complain** [kəm'pleɪn] sich beklagen
could 1 könnte **2** konnte
court [kɔːt]: **tennis court** Tennisplatz
course [kɔːs] Kurs
(to) **cut** [kʌt] schneiden

D

(to) **dare (to)** [deə] wagen (zu)
dinner ['dɪnə] Abendessen
dirty [dɜːti] schmutzig, dreckig
dream [driːm] Traum

E

(to) **earn** [ɜːn] verdienen
earring ['ɪərɪŋ] Ohrring
(to) **empty** ['empti] (ent)leeren
end [end]: **at the end** am Ende
especially [ɪ'speʃəli] besonders
ethnic ['eθnik] ethnisch
everywhere ['evriweə] überall
exactly [ɪg'zæktli] (haar)genau
excited [ɪk'saɪtɪd]: (to) **feel excited** aufgeregt sein
extra ['ekstrə]: **extra hours** Überstunden; **extra money** zusätzlicher Lohn

F

face [feɪs] Gesicht
fair [feə] **1** blond **2** gerecht
fat [fæt] Öl
feeling [fiːlɪŋ] Gefühl
flat [flæt] flach
(to) **flirt** [flɜːt] flirten
floor [flɔː] Fußboden, Boden
fork [fɔːk] Gabel
frying pan ['fraɪŋ pæn] Bratpfanne
furious ['fjʊəriəs] wütend

G

gang [gæŋ] Bande
(to) **go on** weitermachen
good-looking gut aussehend
grey [greɪ] grau
(to) **grow away from** sich entfremden von
grumpy ['grʌmpi] schlecht gelaunt, mürrisch

H

had finished: she had finished sie hatte beendet
hair [heə] Haar
(to) **hammer** ['hæmə] hämmern, laut klopfen
hard-working fleißig
helmet ['helmɪt] Helm
horrible ['hɒrəbl] scheußlich

I

immigrant ['ɪmɪgrənt] Immigrant, Einwanderer
individual [ɪndɪ'vɪdʒuəl] Individuum, einzelne Person
inside [ɪn'saɪd] im; herein; drinnen
(to) **interrupt** [ɪntə'rʌpt] unterbrechen

K

(to) **kiss** [kɪs] küssen
knives (*pl.*) [naɪfz] Messer

L

last [lɑːst]**: at last** endlich; (to) **last** halten; überleben
lay down [lei]**:** *s.p.* (to) **lie down** sich hinlegen
lazy ['leɪzi] faul
leaf [liːf] Blatt
(to) **lie down** [laɪ] sich hinlegen
lifestyle ['laɪfstaɪl] Lebensstil
line [laɪn] Reihe
(to) **load** [ləʊd] einräumen
lost [lɒst]**: if she lost her job** wenn sie ihren Job verlieren würde
love: give my love to viele Grüße an
lunchtime ['lʌntʃtaɪm] mittags

M

(to) **make:** (to) **make oneself at home** sich wie zu Hause fühlen; (to) **make it work** alles tun, damit es funktioniert
message: I get the message ich verstehe
microwave ['maɪkrəweɪv] Mikrowellenherd
mist [mɪst] Nebel; **sea mist** *Nebel, der vom Meer kommt*
mistake [mɪ'steɪk] Fehler
mobile (phone) ['məʊbaɪl 'fəʊn] Handy, Mobiltelefon
moment ['məʊmənt] Moment; **at that moment** in diesem Augenblick; **for a moment** einen Moment lang; **in a moment** gleich
Moors [mɔːz] *hügelige Landschaft in der Nähe von Scarborough*
more: not … any more nicht mehr
motorbike ['məʊtəbaɪk] Motorrad
mouth [maʊθ] Mund

N

neck [nek] Hals
nervous ['nɜ:vəs] nervös
none: none of your business das geht dich nichts an
nonsense ['nɒnsns]**: you're talking nonsense** du erzählst Unsinn

O

once [wʌns] einmal
opinion [ə'pɪnjən] Meinung
order ['ɔ:də] Bestellung; (to) **order** bestellen
origin ['ɒrɪdʒɪn] Herkunft
over: (to) **come over** herüberkommen
(to) **owe** [əʊ] schulden

P

(to) **pack** [pæk] packen
Pakistani [pɑ:kɪ'stɑ:ni] pakistanisch
pan: frying pan ['fraɪŋ pæn] Bratpfanne
parcel ['pɑ:sl] Paket
(to) **pass** [pɑ:s] vorbeigehen, vorbeifahren
past [pɑ:st]**: past some factories** an einigen Fabriken vorbei
phone: on the phone am Telefon
phone call Telefonanruf
photography [fə'tɒgrəfi] Fotografie
piece [pi:s] Stück
(to) **prepare** [prɪ'peə] vorbereiten
(to) **promise** ['prɒmɪs] versprechen
(to) **protest** [prə'test] protestieren

R

racist ['reɪsɪst] **1** rassistisch **2** Rassist/in
rainbow ['reɪnbəʊ] Regenbogen
rang [ræŋ]**:** *s.p.* (to) **ring** klingeln
real ['ri:əl] wirklich
(to) **ride** [raɪd] mit dem Motorrad fahren
(to) **ring** [rɪŋ] klingeln
rocket ['rɒkɪt] Rakete
romantic [rəʊ'mæntɪk] romantisch
(to) **ruin** ['ru:ɪn] ruinieren, zerstören

S

sand [sænd] Sand
sea [si:] Meer
second ['sekənd]**: a second time** ein zweites Mal
(to) **serve** [sɜ:v] bedienen
sexist [seksɪst] frauenfeindlich
shock [ʃɒk] Schock
shocked [ʃɒkt] schockiert
shoulder ['ʃəʊldə] Schulter
simple ['sɪmpl] einfach
single ['sɪŋgl] einzelne
sir [sɜ:] mein Herr (*höfliche Anredeform)*
(to) **sit down** sich setzen
situation [sɪtʃu'eɪʃn] Situation
skin [skɪn] Haut
(to) **slam** [slæm]**:** zuknallen
smell [smel] Geruch, Gestank
(to) **smile** [smaɪl] lächeln
spoon [spu:n] Löffel
spoonful ['spu:nfʊl]**: a spoonful of ice-cream** ein Löffel Eiskrem
(to) **squeeze** [skwi:z] drücken
(to) **stare at** [steə] anstarren
(to) **stir** [stɜ:] umrühren
strange [streɪndʒ] seltsam, komisch
sweet [swi:t] süß
swimming-pool ['swɪmɪŋ pu:l] Schwimmbad

T

tennis court ['tenɪs kɔ:t] Tennisplatz
time: from time to time von Zeit zu Zeit

torn [tɔːn]**:** *p.p.* (to) **tear** zerreißen
transport ['trænspɔːt] Transport(möglichkeit)
trick [trɪk] Trick
twice [twaɪs] zweimal

U
uncooked [ʌn'kʊkt] ungekocht
used to ['juːst tə]**:** (to) **be used to** gewöhnt sein an; (to) **get used to** sich gewöhnen an

V
valley ['væli] Tal
voice [vɔɪs] Stimme

W
waitress ['weɪtrəs] Kellnerin
wave [weɪv] Welle; (to) **wave** winken
well [wel] nun, also
went on: *s.p.* (to) **go on** fortfahren, fortsetzen
(to) **wonder** ['wʌndə] sich überlegen, sich fragen
(to) **work** funktionieren, klappen; (to) **make it work** alles tun, damit es funktioniert
(to) **worry** ['wʌri] sich Sorgen machen; sich Gedanken machen
would [wʊd]**:** **she would** sie würde

After reading: Discussion Points

1 Mrs Croft says: "All teenagers are lazy and stupid."
What do *you* think?

2 There are two other times in the story when somebody says things about a whole group of people. Who is talking about which group of people and what is he/she saying?

3 People sometimes have opinions about people from other countries. What do people sometimes say about Germans? Do you think it's true? Say why/why not?

4 Read the following statements. What do *you* think?
a) Women are less aggressive than men.
b) Women are more emotional than men.
c) Women worry more about what they look like than men.
d) Women are more tidy than men.
e) Men understand science better than women.
f) Men are better at making and repairing things than women.
g) Men don't talk as much as women.
h) Men can read maps better than women.